Saving the Heart

What is an Evangelical?

by Mark Thompson

St Matthias Press

Sydney • London • Capetown

Saving the Heart
© St Matthias Press, 1995

St Matthias Press
PO Box 665
LONDON SW20 8RU
ENGLAND
Tel: (081) 947 5658 Fax: (081) 944 7091

ISBN 1 873166 12 5

The articles in this booklet have been reprinted from the *The Briefing* a
periodical produced by St Matthias Press 22 times a year. Annual subscrip-
tion costs £12.50. To order, please call 0181-947 5686

Contents

1 Foundations

THESE DAYS, IT SEEMS, everyone wants to be an 'evangelical'.

It is a label being worn by an increasing number of Christians from diverse backgrounds and with varying beliefs. In a move that would have seemed impossible even 30 years ago, today some Roman Catholics rejoice to be known as 'evangelical Catholics'.

However, calling yourself 'evangelical' has not always been so popular.

The word itself comes from the Greek word for 'gospel'. Martin Luther shocked the Christian world in 1519, when he described as "altogether Christian and evangelical" some of the teachings of Jan Hus, a Bohemian theologian who had been condemned and burnt at the stake in 1415. Later it was the only label Luther would accept for his own teaching. Sir Thomas More is generally recognized as the man who brought the word into the English language. In the course of a quite vitriolic attack on William Tyndale in 1532, More spoke of 'those evangelicalles'.

In the centuries since the Reformation, 'evangelicals' have had a chequered history. At various times they have been strong, such as during the 'evangelical awakenings' under the Wesleys and Whitefield. At other times, they have been something of a persecuted minority.

These days, however, evangelicalism seems to be carrying all before it. A spate of recent books and articles has chronicled its growth as a force within Christendom. Evangelical Christianity is making people sit up and take notice. Evangelical churches are growing, unlike many of their 'liberal' and 'high church' counterparts. Evangelical colleges and seminaries are full. Evangelical bishops are now found in growing numbers in mainline denominations. Evangelicalism's star is in the ascendant—so many people are claiming.

However, behind the hype, the citations of statistics and the self-congratulation, not all is as it seems. With the recent growth and success of evangelicalism, and the 'bandwagon effect' of people climbing aboard, confusion is growing about just what it means to be an 'evangelical'. The danger facing us today is a steady theological drift, as more and more people claim the label 'evangelical' for themselves, even though they hold widely differing beliefs. The term 'evangelical' is increasingly being used to describe a party or sociological group, or a sense of warm personal piety, rather than any particular set of beliefs.

Genuine evangelicalism can only be defined by its core beliefs. Evangelicals are those whose beliefs and practice are shaped by the gospel of Jesus Christ. We are unavoidably cross-centred people, for the gospel *is* the declaration of Christ's atoning death on the cross, and his victorious resurrection with its summons to faith and a life of discipleship. Evangelicals are just as clearly *Bible* people, for our knowledge of the gospel arises from the pages of Holy Scripture. Attempts to define evangelicalism in other ways—in terms of sociology or spirituality—will always distort the picture.

This commitment to the biblical gospel also explains why evangelicalism is not satisfied with being described as one particular brand of Christianity. Don Carson put it like this:

> Until about twenty or thirty years ago, evangelicalism, in its various cycles of strength and weakness, was nevertheless characterised by a clear, strong insistence on the basic elements of Christianity that have always characterised the Christian church when it has been virulent. And there was the notion that, properly understood, evangelicalism was not one branch of the church, but is the church returning to basics; it is the church returning to the purest and sim-

plest form of the gospel; it is the church at its straightforward best.

But today we find the borders of evangelicalism changing... At the very point when evangelicalism has again grown quite considerably over the last forty years, it has in fact lost its heart.[1]

John Stott said much the same thing back in 1970:

It is the contention of evangelicals that they are plain Bible Christians, and that in order to be a biblical Christian it is necessary to be an evangelical Christian[2]

Statements like these raise the stakes enormously when we come to explain just what is an evangelical. We are not simply defining an interesting and distinctive group within the Christian spectrum; we are defining authentic, biblical Christianity. Evangelical theology is not simply our label; it is God's truth for the world.

Of course, there is a danger in too much definition. An obsession with self-definition is a recipe for disaster. It is possible to spend so much time describing what evangelicals believe and practise that no time is left to believe and practise. We can become inward-looking and inactive, so concerned with doctrinal purity that we never preach the gospel.

As I have already suggested, however, *lack* of clear definition is the danger facing us today. Evangelicalism is losing its heart. As is necessary from time to time, we need to call each other back to the foundations of evangelical Christianity.

And so to this booklet. It is designed to outline what genuine evangelicalism is. The chapters take up the major doctrines which shape evangelical belief and show you how they come from the Bible. Following each chapter is a short optional study section which you can do in a group or on your own.

What is an evangelical?

Evangelical belief and practice comes from the gospel of Jesus Christ. It is based on the grand rescue mission of God, which is

1. In an interview in P. D. Jensen and T. Payne, "Have Evangelicals lost their way?" (St Matthias Press/Lancer, 1991), p.42.

2. J.R.W. Stott, "Christ the controversialist: A study in some essentials of the evangelical religion." (London: Tyndale, 1970), 32.

the theme of both the Old Testament and the New.

We are going to look at six fundamental ideas that are the basis of evangelical theology, beginning with the source of all our knowledge about theology: the Bible.

Point 1: Evangelicals have a distinctive view of revelation

Being committed to the gospel means being commited to the authority of Scripture. Not only is the gospel made known to us in these very pages, but Christ himself believed in the authority of Scripture. Jesus explained himself and his work in terms of God's purposes revealed in the Old Testament. He also looked forward to the writing of the New Testament when he spoke of the Spirit enabling the apostles to remember all that he had told them (Jn 14:26) and when he prayed for those who would believe through the word of the apostles (Jn 17:20). His commission and authorization stands behind the ministry of the apostles and their writing. In the end, any attempt to separate the gospel of Jesus Christ and the Bible will distort both, for the God of the gospel is the God of the Bible (2 Cor 4:6), and the gospel itself is the central theme of the whole Bible (Lk 24:27).

This collection of books is not just an expression of human ideas, nor is it simply a record of human religious beliefs or experiences. The Bible is the living and active Word of God. What the Bible says, God says, and those who have been rescued by God recognize his voice (1 Th 2:13; Jn 10:1-18).

This is the Bible's own testimony about itself. An evangelical doctrine of the Word of God really begins in Genesis 1, where God speaks and the universe comes into being. The words that God speaks are not just ordinary words. They are powerful and creative, expressing God's mind and purpose. They always accomplish what he intends (Isa 55:8-11). It comes as no surprise, then, that when God becomes a man, he stills storms with a word (Mk 4:35-41), casts out demons with a word (Mk 5:1-20), heals the sick with a word (Mk 1:40-44) and even raises the dead with a word (Mk 5:35-43). God speaks and it is so.

God himself commanded his word to be written down. He decreed it to be the authoritative guide for his people, and the standard by which they make judgements. In fact, God himself was the first to present his word in written form (Ex 31:18). In these written words God confronted his people, challenging them and comforting them as directly and effectively as when he spoke to Moses in the cloud. They are not merely a *record* of God's self-revelation—they *are* that revelation.

God also used human writers in the process. The divine authority and reliability of the Scriptures is in no way diminished by this fact. God does not by-pass the mind or personality of each writer, for those things too are his creation. Through the work of his Spirit, God enables them to write *his* word, not just their own (2 Pet 1:20-21★). This is not only true of the Old Testament, as is clear from the way Jesus refers to it (e.g. Matt 19:4-5), but of the New Testament as well. Even while the apostles were still alive and writing, their words were recognized as Scripture (2 Pet 3:15-16; see also 1 Tim 5:18, where the second Scripture quotation is not found in the Old Testament, but is a saying of Jesus recorded in Luke 10:7).

2 Timothy 3:14-17★ appears against this background. This is the classic statement of Scripture about itself. Given that the New Testament writings were recognised at the time as Scripture, it cannot be restricted to the Old Testament alone. In the context of a threat from false teaching, Paul speaks of the *sufficiency* of Scripture. These writings are unique, Paul says, for they come from the mouth of God and are God's full and sufficient provision to equip Christians *thoroughly* for life as the rescued children of God.

The Scriptures, then, are the unique source of our knowledge of God. Only in the light of the Scriptures can we understand how the heavens declare the glory of God. Only in the light of the Scriptures can we understand the reason for the ambiguities of life. Only in the Scriptures can we discern the mind of God and the seriousness of his love towards us.

For this reason the Scriptures must stand above every other pronouncement on matters of faith and practice. This does not mean we cannot think hard and creatively about the implications

Above all, you must understand that no prophecy of Scripture came about by the prophet's own interpretation. For prophecy never had its origin in the will of man, but men spoke from God as they were carried along by the Holy Spirit. (2 Pet 1:20-21).

But as for you, continue in what you have learned and have become convinced of, because you know those from whom you learned it, and how from infancy you have known the holy Scriptures, which are able to make you wise for salvation through faith in Christ Jesus. All Scripture is God-breathed, and is useful for teaching, rebuking, correcting and training in righteousness, so that the man of God may be thoroughly equipped for every good work. (2 Tim 3:14-17)

9

of the Christian gospel. Nor does it mean that every other piece of theological writing is untrue. Biblical Christians have always read and written things other than the Bible. Luther, the great champion of *sola Scriptura* (Scripture alone), regularly quoted the church fathers, especially Augustine. But Luther and other biblical Christians measured such writings by the teaching of Holy Scripture. Nothing has the right to bind the Christian conscience except Scripture alone. Where Christian teaching or human reason or even personal experience conflict with Scripture, they are to be rejected. The Bible settles the matter.

This must apply to evangelical theology itself, as John Stott made clear:

> Certainly it is the desire of evangelicals to be neither more nor less than biblical Christians. Their intention is not to be partisan, that is, they do not cling to certain tenets for the sake of maintaining their identity as a 'party'. On the contrary, they have always expressed their readiness to modify, even abandon, any or all of their cherished beliefs if they can be shown to be unbiblical.[3]

3. Stott, ibid., p. 32.

If this is true, something follows which is not particularly popular at the moment. If biblical truth matters, and if we genuinely care for our evangelical brothers and sisters, then we will be prepared to challenge them when they stray from that truth. Solomon's words are more true than we often recognize: "Wounds from a friend can be trusted, but an enemy multiplies kisses" (Prov 27:6).

Study Guide

Review

What does 'evangelical' mean?

Why do we say that 'genuine evangelicalism can only be defined by its core beliefs'?

Why can we not accept that evangelicalism is just one brand of Christianity?

Why do we regard Scripture as the final authority?

Investigate

How is the word of God active today? (Heb 4:12-13)

How are the Old and New Testaments tied together? (Luke 24:27)

How would you describe the relationship between God as author and the human authors? (2 Pet 1:20-21; 2 Pet 3:15)

Think it Through

Why does nothing else but Scripture have the right to bind our conscience?

If God is the author of Scripture, what should be our attitude to it?

What rival authorities to God speaking in Scripture present themselves to us? How should we deal with them?

The problem
and its solution

We have seen so far that evangelicals have a distinctive view of revelation. Now we build on that basis with the next two of the six fundamental ideas of evangelicalism.

Point 2: Evangelicals have a distinctive view of human nature

Evangelicals believe that sin is a serious problem. In fact, the gospel is good news precisely because of the seriousness of sin. The rescue mission of God would make no sense if there was no danger from which we need to be rescued. The death of Jesus would be a barbaric over-reaction on God's part if that danger could be averted in any other way. The entire Bible testifies that every human being is in a very real and serious danger of his or her own making.

This greatest of all dangers facing men and women is long-standing. It originated with the decisions of the first man and woman to disobey God and grasp the opportunity of moral independence (Gen 3). They wanted to decide for themselves what was right and wrong without depending upon the word of God. They chose not to trust God. It was a fundamentally self-centred and self-seeking decision. As Genesis 3 and indeed the rest of the Bible make clear, its consequences were devastating. The entire human race shares in their corruption and guilt, for from our earliest moments we are all predisposed to make the same choice. We set ourselves up as the rulers of our lives (Rom 5:12). Every man, woman and child is biased towards sin (Rom 3:23).

Our sin alienates us from God and makes us his enemies (Isa

Once you were alienated from God and were enemies in your minds because of your evil behaviour. (Col 1:21).

It is a dreadful thing to fall into the hands of the living God. (Heb 10:31).

59:1-2; Col 1:21★). It provokes the coming wrath of God (Rom 1:18-32; Col 3:5-6). In the face of our guilt and corruption, the prospect of judgement is terrifying (Heb 9:27; 10:31★).

The problem is made worse because there is nothing we can do about it. The Bible uses two key pictures to show our inability to save ourselves. The first is slavery—the natural human condition is slavery to sin (Rom 6). The second picture is death: apart from Christ we are dead in our sins (Eph 2:1). There is a world of difference between 'sick' and 'dead'. The former suggests some possibility of recovery; the latter brings an end to all such hopes. If we are to be rescued from the danger we are in, it will not be by our own doing. The initiative must come from outside.

Our most basic needs are forgiveness and reconciliation with God. Any attempt to modify this understanding of our character will lead to a different gospel and a different ministry. Although evangelicals have made significant contributions in areas such as justice for the oppressed, international peace, and environmental awareness, they have steadfastly maintained that these are not the gospel. A theological preoccupation with such goals inevitably leads to a confusion about the plight of humankind. The Bible takes us beyond the symptoms to the disease.

Point 3: Evangelicals have a distinctive view of salvation

If the foundation of evangelical theology is the authority of the Scripture, the central point of evangelical theology is the cross of Jesus Christ. By his death Jesus makes the atonement which deals with our sin and restores us to God. He dies in our place, bearing the penalty for our sin, in line with God's ancient intention. Here we see the most profound demonstration of God's love for us.

This saving act of God in Christ is in view from the very earliest pages of the Bible. The promise of a full, final and effective solution to the problem of sin holds the Bible together and propels the Old Testament into the New. This promise is unfolded gradually, beginning with barely more than the hint of a promised deliverer who will suffer in the process of rescuing God's rebellious creation (Gen 3:15★). It climaxes in the prophetic announcement of the Suffering Servant who takes upon himself "the iniquity of us all" and bears "the punishment that brought us peace" (Isa 53). Along the way important anticipations of the atonement in and through Jesus are given in the Exodus and Passover narratives (Ex 11–12) and amongst the Psalms (e.g. Ps 22).

> And I will put enmity between you and the woman and between your offspring and hers;
> he will crush your head, and you will strike his heel.
> (Gen 3:15).

The anticipation is answered in the New Testament. John the Baptist's testimony to Jesus was against the background of the Old Testament promises. As Jesus came towards him, John declared, "Look, the lamb of God, who takes away the sin of the world" (Jn 1:29).

Jesus also described his mission in these terms: he came to serve and to be a "ransom for many" (Mk 10:45★). He took on the mission of the Suffering Servant, deliberately applying Isaiah 53 to himself in Luke 22:37. He was the one who would accomplish at last the atonement for which the whole Old Testament had been waiting.

> For even the Son of Man did not come to be served, but to serve, and to give his life as a ransom for many.
> (Mk 10:45).

The testimony of the apostles follows on from that of Jesus. When the apostles speak of the atonement by Jesus' death on the cross, they appeal to Old Testament images and categories to explain this great event, just as Jesus did. Jesus died in our place and bore the curse of God for us (2 Cor 5:21; Gal 3:13; 1 Pet 3:18★; 1 Jn 2:2).

> For Christ died for sins once for all, the righteous for the unrighteous, to bring you to God.
> (1 Pet 3:18).

At the heart of the atonement is Jesus' death in our place, a death which involves bearing the penalty for our sin. All the other things we know about the cross only make sense if we understand this. Jesus' death is an example of self-sacrificial love only when we realise that he died in our place, taking our sin. Jesus' death is a victory over death and the devil *because* he has dealt with sin and so taken the sting out of death (1 Cor 15:56) and broken the hold of the devil (Heb 2:14–15). Here is God's most profound answer to the human dilemma. This is what makes the gospel such good news.

Study Guide

Investigate

Read Romans 1:18-32; 2:12; 3:9-23; 5:12-14; 6:16-18.
What is sin?

Who sins?

What are the consequences of sin?

Think it Through

How does this view of the human problem differ from other religions?

Why are we unable to remedy our own problem of sin?

What difference would it make to Christianity if we had a different view of sin?

Investigate

Read Isaiah 53, Mark 10:45, Luke 22:37
How did Jesus view himself and his ministry?

Read Romans 3:21-26; 5:6-10; 2 Cor 5:14-15; 21
How does Jesus' death answer the human dilemma?

Why would any other solution be inadequate?

Think it Through

Why do we need to understand sin before we can understand why Jesus died?

3   Our saved life

In this chapter, we finish our study of the six basic points of evangelicalism as we look at Christian response to the gospel, the work of the Spirit, and what we can expect in the future.

Point 4: Evangelicals have a distinctive view of Christian response

The gospel of Jesus Christ is both an announcement and a summons—the announcement of God's intervention to save us and a summons to respond with faith. This idea of promise and trust describes the way in which God relates to his people throughout the Old Testament (Heb 11). The most obvious example is Abraham. When God announced his intention to give Abraham a son, an intention which considering his and his wife's age seemed improbable (to say the least), we are told "Abram believed the Lord, and he credited it to him as righteousness" (Gen 15:6). Abraham was not perfect, as the succeeding chapters of Genesis show quite clearly. He could not and he did not earn God's favour. But God was worth trusting. What he promised to do he would do. Abraham knew that, and he responded by trusting God. God declares that response to be righteousness.

Throughout the Old Testament the promise of salvation points to the future. The search for the seed of the woman, which began

back in Genesis 3, drives us from the Old Testament into the
New. None of the great figures of faith in the Old Testament
actually received what had been promised (Heb 11:39★). They
died in faith, trusting that the fulfilment was still to come. God
had promised and they believed him. They, like Abraham, were
right with God.

Jesus appears against this background, as the fulfilment of God's
promises and the object of faith. He stands in stark contrast to the
performance-oriented Judaism of the time, which was a grotesque
mutation of the covenantal faith of the Old Testament. He exer-
cises an authority to forgive sin on the earth in unexpected direc-
tions (Mk 2:10). He is happy to be described as "a friend of tax
collectors and sinners" (Lk 7:34). His controversial parable about
a Pharisee and a tax collector exposes how hopeless it is to relate
to God on the basis of performance (Lk 18:7-14). The tax collector, who had nothing to plead before God, "went home justified
before God" (Lk 18:14). The Pharisee, with all his boasts, did
not. At Jesus' death, those who trumpet their own righteousness
mock him, while those who recognize that their only hope lies in
him hear the words of forgiveness and assurance (Lk 23:40-43).

Paul's teaching on justification carries on from the ministry of
Jesus. God is the one who "justifies the ungodly" (Rom 4:5★). A
right standing with God comes not through religious performance but through the faithfulness of Jesus Christ (cf Rom 3:22).
Those who put their trust in Jesus are right with God and need
no longer fear the prospect of condemnation (Rom 8:1-4). Our
new standing with God is not our own invention; it is his declaration in the face of the atonement made by Jesus on the cross and
our faith in him (Rom 3:22-26).

'Justification by faith alone' is a slogan which reflects the New
Testament teaching of justification apart from works of the law
(Rom 3:28). It safeguards the Christian insistence that our boast
lies in God alone (1 Cor 1:30-31). However, nowhere in the
New Testament or the Old is there the suggestion that this is the
end of the matter. Genuine faith changes lives. In the matter of
salvation, faith stands alone as our appropriate response to what
God has done. Nevertheless, genuine faith is never alone. Living

faith is bound to reveal itself in repentance and embracing a new life as God's children. The biblical insistence on faith alone does not change the biblical concern for godliness in the life of the believer. Rather, it places that concern in its proper context (Rom 6; Jas 2).

Throughout Christian history, gospel-minded men and women have remarked on the importance of justification by faith alone. This doctrine plays a pivotal role in Christian theology. It reminds us that God initiates salvation. It undermines all human boasting. It focuses our attention on Christ and his cross rather than our performance.

In recent years, some very sophisticated attempts have been made to modify this doctrine, and to displace it from the centre of evangelical theology. Scholars associated with the 'New Perspective' on Paul have argued variously that 'justification by faith' is a peculiarly Pauline doctrine, that it is restricted to his concern for Jew–Gentile relations and that it is more about corporate covenant membership than individual standing with God.

However, evangelicals are bound to point out that, whatever the covenantal background or context, Paul remains deeply concerned over the fate of the individual before God. His teaching about the way God 'justifies the ungodly' reflects, as we have seen, the teaching of the whole Bible, and is embodied in the ministry of Jesus himself.

Point 5: Evangelicals have a distinctive view of grace and the Spirit

Jesus' death and resurrection remains the one and only basis for our acceptance with God. We are called to respond to that marvellous provision by repentance and faith. Such a response does not come naturally to human beings who are trapped in the slavery and death of sin, both guilty and corrupt. God must work a miracle within us, creating the very things which cannot be produced from the depths of a dead and enslaved heart.

John's Gospel emphasizes this human inability to believe without the miraculous intervention of God. Christians are not chil-

In reply Jesus declared, "I tell you the truth, no one can see the kingdom of God unless he is born again."

"How can a man be born when he is old?" Nicodemus asked. "Surely he cannot enter a second time into his mother's womb to be born!"

Jesus answered, "I tell you the truth, no one can enter the kingdom of God unless he is born of water and the Spirit." (Jn 3:3-5).

Take the helmet of salvation and the sword of the Spirit, which is the word of God. (Eph 6:17).

dren of God by virtue of a human decision (Jn 1:12-13); rather, through the work of God's Spirit, they must be "born again" (Jn 3:3,5★). The use of imagery from Ezekiel 36 in Jesus' conversation with Nicodemus reminds us that this 'new birth' has always been God's intention.

This teaching of Jesus is highly significant, for it reveals that both the outward and inward aspects of salvation are the work of God. God has provided the atonement in Christ, and God has brought us to new birth by his Spirit in order that we might enjoy the benefits of Christ's atonement. Christians stand as grateful recipients of a full and final salvation, not as its initiators or contributors.

That is the most basic evangelical understanding of the work of the Spirit. In recent years some have suggested that evangelicalism has ignored the Holy Spirit. This is simply not true. The person and work of the Holy Spirit have never been neglected by evangelical writers. Evangelicals have always maintained the significance of the Spirit in creation, redemption and the life of the church. They have always spoken of the Spirit's vital role in the greatest miracle of all: bringing a person from death to life. We refuse to trivialize the work of the Spirit or to ignore the fact that the sword of the Spirit is the Word of God (Eph 6:17★). The Christian response to God's mercy in Christ is impossible without the work of the Spirit: the new birth. The Christian life is life in the Spirit. Personal conversion is the outward manifestation of this inward reality.

This is precisely why evangelical theology cannot be described as abstract or merely intellectual. It is profoundly experiential. It recognises that the beginning of the Christian life is the experience of new birth brought about by the Spirit of God. So while evangelicalism can only be defined theologically, its theology is intensely practical, proclaiming the direct personal address of the living God to one made alive by the Holy Spirit.

Point 6: Evangelicals have a distinctive view of the future

The gospel call to repentance and faith is urgent because of the future reality guaranteed by the resurrection of Jesus from the dead. God has "set a day when he will judge the world with justice by the man he has appointed. He has given proof of this to all men by raising him from the dead" (Acts 17:31). The finale of human and universal history will be the creation of a new heavens and a new earth (Rev 21:1), but this will be preceded by the judgement of all men and women (Rev 20:11-15). In the light of these realities, Christians can be described as those who have "turned to God from idols to serve the living and true God, and to wait for his Son from heaven, whom he raised from the dead— Jesus, who rescues us from the coming wrath" (1 Thess 1:9-10).

There are a variety of views, even within evangelicalism, on the timing and precise nature of the events leading up to the final judgement. In part, these arise from our difficulties in understanding the apocalyptic language of the Book of Revelation. Nevertheless, the personal return of the glorified Lord Jesus and the reality of universal judgement are beyond dispute. The only hope of rescue lies in Jesus Christ himself. This sure and certain rescue takes the fear out of the future for the Christian and makes the promise of Jesus' return a message of comfort (1 Thess 4:13-18).

Such a view of the future carries with it a view of the present. The New Testament is full of warnings that Jesus' return will be swift and unexpected (1 Thess 5:1-11; Rev 22:7). It also presents us with the reason for an interval between Jesus' ascension and return: "The Lord is not slow in keeping his promise, as some understand slowness. He is patient with you, not wanting anyone to perish, but everyone to come to repentance" (2 Pet 3:9). The present time is an opportunity for repentance and faith. The end of all things is delayed so that others might be included in the great Rescue. That is God's great concern for the present age. As those already rescued, it should also be our great concern.

It is no surprise then that *evangelism* is at the forefront of evangelical practice. This commitment springs not only from our view of the future and the present, but also from our understanding of the Bible, sin, the work of Christ and the necessity of faith and new birth by the Spirit. God's kindness in rescuing us through Christ creates in us a desire to see others rescued too. Judgement is real, and God's mercy in Jesus is great. These combine as a most powerful motivation for evangelistic ministry (2 Cor 5:11–21).

Study Guide

Review

Why is it important to remember that God initiates salvation?

How does the doctrine of the atoning sacrifice of Jesus lead to a doctrine of justification by faith alone?

Investigate

Read Romans 5:1-11

How does justification by faith alone make us sure of salvation?

What is our present state before God?

What is the connection between our present state and our future?

Read Titus 3:3-7

What ideas here are similar to those in Romans 5:1-11?

What role does the Holy Spirit have in salvation?

How do we receive the Holy Spirit?

What is the result of having the Holy Spirit?

Read 1 Thessalonians 1:9-10; 2 Thessalonians 1:5-10; 2 Peter 3:9

In what ways will our beliefs about the future affect the present?

What are our reasons for evangelism?

Why has the judgement day not come yet?

Think it Through

What view of the present would you have if you believed in
　　—reincarnation?

　　　　—materialism (there is nothing after death)?

How is the work of Jesus connected with the work of the Spirit?

If someone responded to 'justification by faith alone' by saying, "Well, does that mean you can molest children and just ask for forgiveness?"—what would you answer?

4

Love and
Evangelicalism

Evangelical theology makes sense

These six fundamental perspectives are not all that could be said about evangelical theology. Evangelicals have much to say about the Trinity, creation and the church, amongst many other things. This booklet has not been intended as an exercise in determining the *minimum* one must believe to be considered an evangelical. These six biblical truths, however, give evangelicalism its basic shape.

All the truths are woven together in the gospel of Jesus Christ and founded upon Scripture. It made sense, then, that we examined the doctrine of Scripture first. God explains to us in Scripture our own predicament—our sinfulness and our need for judgement. Once we know this, the solution to our problem—Jesus' atoning death on our behalf—makes perfect sense. Jesus alone can save us out of sin. Our response is to turn back from our former way of life and to trust in the promise—and even that comes from the regenerating work of the Spirit in us. Finally, knowing that Jesus *has* died for us, we have confidence in the future, and wait in expectation for Jesus' return. These are the fundamental truths. Any change in theology at these critical points is a shift from evangelicalism.

In today's climate such changes rarely take the form of outright denial. The more dangerous (and sadly more frequent) modification comes through *addition*. This has always been the case. Evangelical theology is often summarized by the slogans 'Scripture alone', 'Christ alone', 'Grace alone' and 'Faith alone'. Jim Packer echoed their concerns when he wrote:

> You cannot add to evangelical theology without subtracting from it. By augmenting it, you cannot enrich it; you can only impoverish it. Thus, for example, if you add to it a doctrine of human priestly mediation you take away the truth of the perfect adequacy of our Lord's priestly mediation. If you add to it a doctrine of human merit, in whatever form, you take away the truth of the merits of Christ... The principle applies at point after point. What is more than evangelical is less than evangelical. Evangelical theology, by its very nature, cannot be supplemented; it can only be denied.[1]

1. J.I. Packer, "The Evangelical Anglican Identity Problem: An Analysis", Latimer Studies 1 (Oxford: Latimer, 1978), pp 17-18.

Put another way, the crucial questions are ones of sufficiency. Is the Bible sufficient as the saving revelation of God? Evangelicals have answered 'yes' to this question; those outside the evangelical tradition have supplemented the Bible with human reason, church pronouncements, or private visions, dreams and prophetic statements. Is Jesus' death sufficient to deal with our sins and secure our relationship with God? Again evangelicals have answered 'yes', while non-evangelicals have argued that the activities of the church play a role in this as well. Is faith sufficient as the appropriate response to the offer of forgiveness? The evangelical 'yes' to this question stands in stark contrast to the imposition of works, or ceremonies, or second experiences.

Room to move

Evangelicalism, even when defined in terms of its distinctives, is not entirely without diversity. Outside of these distinctives there is room for difference and even disagreement without resorting to rejecting one another. The fundamental doctrines of evangelical theology ought to inform the way we handle such points of difference.

Some points of difference arise on matters about which the

Bible is largely, and in some cases completely, silent. The decisions about when and how to baptize seem to fall into this category. While good cases can be mounted for both infant and adult baptism, the fact is that the Bible says little about baptism in relation to the children of believers. The appropriate evangelical response to such differences is to recognize the issues as matters of Christian freedom. We have no right to bind the consciences of other believers in ways that the Scriptures do not. We might hold firmly to our own view as a legitimate expression of biblical principles. Nevertheless, it is a mistake to invest those views with the same authority as the teaching of Scripture.

Another kind of difference is when we disagree over what precisely the Bible is saying on a given issue it addresses. Our commitment to the truth and authority of Scripture demands a quite different response in these cases. Because understanding what God has to say on the issue is so important, and because we acknowledge that our hearts and minds are sinful, evangelicals are committed to dialogue and the repeated re-examination of the passages in question. This is not always easy because it involves admitting that we may have misunderstood what a particular passage is saying. Nevertheless, the truth is more important than maintaining a position or winning an argument. Sometimes, the questions of a critic are an important step along the way to a clearer understanding of just what the Bible is saying.

Love and truth

Evangelicalism can only be defined in relation to the gospel of Jesus Christ because 'evangelical' is simply another way of saying 'biblical Christian'. Yet this is a dangerous business. It alienates those who, for whatever reason, wish to retain the label while 'growing out of' its basic beliefs. It raises the question of theological truth and implies that other Christian traditions (catholic, charismatic, liberal) involve some kind of error. Surely, some have argued, it would be more loving to define evangelicalism in another way, one which would allow us to soften those distinctions and embrace the ecumenical spirit.

In the last few years, attempts to do this have been made; attempts to go beyond a theological definition of evangelicalism. Using a much broader brush than I have in this booklet, it is possible to paint a rosy picture of the onward march of evangelicals and a new golden age for the church. What was once seen as theological difference is now being cherished as diversity. We are told that mature evangelicalism rejoices in its new-found diversity, discovering brotherhood in the most unlikely of places. A new positive outlook has replaced the negativity which characterised evangelicalism for so long.

Yet the sad truth is that if we redefine what we believe in this way, the result is an evangelicalism with no heart. Evangelicalism must not surrender to a caricature of itself as narrow-minded and negative. It must not obligingly change itself into a bland entity which stands for nothing and only smiles when its most cherished beliefs are compromised. We must never forget that genuine Christian unity is unity in the *truth*. We do not aim for a *balance* of love and truth; rather, *both* love and truth. Love built on a lie is not love at all and stands opposed to the purposes of God in both the Old and New Testaments. God shows his love for us in that while we were still sinners, Christ died for us. If we forget any part of the truth of the gospel, we run the risk of forgetting what it is to love.

The heart of genuine evangelicalism is the gospel of the Lord Jesus Christ. This gospel is the only hope for a world heading towards judgement. Evangelicals must faithfully guard the gospel, and cannot afford to be distracted from its proclamation. Our distinctive theological framework urges us to this task. In the final analysis, we show evangelicalism to be right by the salvation of men and women who have heard the truth and believed.

Study Guide

Review

Why does adding to evangelical theology subtract from it?

Can you think of some examples where this has occurred?

How do we decide what to do with issues on which the Bible is silent?

How can we tell what is fundamental to biblical belief and what is a matter of freedom? Think of some examples that might come up in church.

How can we keep ourselves from reading our own ideas and preferences into the Bible, instead of reading God's ideas from the Bible?

Investigate

Read Ephesians 4:11-16
What are the marks of Christian maturity?

What sort of unity should we aim for?

What part does love play? How does it relate to truth and error?

Think it Through

Why is diversity so attractive?

Why is ecumenism (all brands of Christianity joining together regardless of doctrinal differences) not, in the end, loving?